MW00814497

core belief™

Bible Study Series
for senior high

WHY God's Justice MATTERS

Group

Loveland, Colorado

Why God's Justice Matters
Core Belief Bible Study Series
Copyright © 1997 Group Publishing, Inc.

All rights reserved. No part of this book may be reproduced in any manner whatsoever without prior written permission from the publisher, except where noted in the text and in the case of brief quotations embodied in critical articles and reviews. For information, write Permissions, Group Publishing, Inc., Dept. BK, P.O. Box 481, Loveland, CO 80539.

Credits
Editors: Debbie Gowensmith and Lisa Baba Lauffer
Creative Development Editor: Paul Woods
Chief Creative Officer: Joani Schultz
Copy Editor: Helen Turnbull
Art Directors: Bill Fisher and Ray Tollison
Cover Art Director: Jeff Storm
Computer Graphic Artist: Ray Tollison
Photographer: Craig DeMartino
Production Manager: Gingar Kunkel

Unless otherwise noted, Scriptures taken from the HOLY BIBLE, NEW INTERNATIONAL VERSION®. Copyright © 1973, 1978, 1984 by International Bible Society. Used by permission of Zondervan Publishing House. All rights reserved.

ISBN 0-7644-0886-0

10 9 8 7 6 5 4 3 2 1   06 05 04 03 02 01 00 99 98 97

Printed in the United States of America.

Bible Study Series
for senior high

contents:

the Core Belief: ▼God's Justice

Young people of every generation have at some time exclaimed, "Life's not fair!" But with just a *human* understanding of justice, those young people—and all of us—improperly perceive justice and injustice in the world.

Justice is the right and impartial treatment of others, and God is unique in his ability to determine justice—he set the standard and sees all things. He governs the world with justice. Because humans are sinful, our injustice separates us from God. But since God is merciful in addition to being just, he provides a way for us to have a relationship with him. Yet someone had to pay the price for our injustice: God punished Jesus Christ, the only sinless human ever to live, for our sins.

Yes, life's not fair. And aren't we lucky!

the ▼Helpful Stuff

the ▼Studies

▼God's Justice as a Core Christian Belief

When it comes to understanding God's justice, your young people face two dangers. They may fall into the belief that justice is simply a matter of opinion and that objective standards of right and wrong don't exist. Or they may look at the world's injustice and fall into despair because they see no way to overcome it. Fortunately, teenagers can avoid both pitfalls by learning what the Bible teaches about God's justice.

The more your young people learn about God, the more they'll see matters of justice from God's perspective. They'll understand that God loves justice and is committed to making the world a just place. With that understanding, your kids can go into the world as agents of God's justice, certain they're on the winning side.

This study course will help your kids develop a clear image of God's justice. First your kids will learn that there *is* a clear, unfaltering, and objective standard for **right and wrong.** They'll discover that God set the standard for justice and revealed that standard in his Word.

In the second study, kids will focus on **injustice** by contrasting God's justice with our culture's sense of fairness. Through this contrast, kids will discover that God's justice is reliable and eternal.

In the third study, which deals with **AIDS,** kids will experience first-hand how their judgments are limited by their perceptions. This study encourages kids to leave judgment to God, who is the only one who can see everyone's heart clearly.

Finally, the fourth study encourages kids to use what they've learned about God's justice—as revealed in Scripture—to make decisions in their lives. As kids explore **civil disobedience,** they'll learn that God's sense of justice does not just deal with their action, but also their inaction.

God continues to establish justice in spite of our sin. He restrains the forces of injustice today and promises to institute perfect justice in the future. In spite of what we sometimes feel, God always has been and always will be just. And because God is just and loves justice, we should commit ourselves to being agents of God's justice in the world.

*For a more comprehensive look at this Core Christian Belief, read Group's **Get Real: Making Core Christian Beliefs Relevant to Teenagers.***

DEPTH FINDER

To help you effectively guide your kids toward this Core Christian Belief, use these overviews as a launching point for a more in-depth study of God's justice.

● **Justice is the right and impartial treatment of others.** An action is right when it follows God's moral standard. That means we must treat one another the way God wants us to—without favoritism or prejudice (Deuteronomy 16:18-20; Psalm 82:3-4; and James 2:1-4).

● **God's character sets the standard of justice.** We don't have the authority to decide what's right and what's wrong. Instead, God's nature determines how we should act toward one another (Deuteronomy 1:16-17; 10:17-18; Matthew 5:48; and Revelation 15:3-4).

● **God governs the world with justice.** Even though we may feel that God has treated us unfairly, God always acts justly. However, God's justice may, on occasion, be delayed or hidden. And sometimes bad things happen—infants die, good people suffer—not because God is unjust, but because we live in a sin-cursed world (Deuteronomy 32:4; Nehemiah 9:33; Zephaniah 3:5; and Romans 3:25b-26).

● **God's justice takes several forms.** God promotes justice by giving equitable laws and ethical guidelines. God also provides various leaders whose responsibility it is to uphold the standards he provides. God also motivates individuals to act justly by rewarding righteousness and punishing sin (Leviticus 19:35-37; Job 38:12-15; Matthew 13:49-50; and Romans 1:18-19; 7:12; 13:1).

● **God balances justice with mercy to forgive human sin.** If God were only just, he would have to condemn us all for our sin. However, God chose to punish his own Son, Jesus, for our sin. As a result, God was able to extend mercy to us without compromising the demands of justice (Isaiah 46:12-13; 51:5; Romans 3:21-26; and 1 John 1:9).

● **Our injustice separates us from God.** Since God is just, he demands the same from us. When we cheat, lie, or take advantage of others, we sin and break our fellowship with God (Isaiah 1:16-20; 59:2-8; Jeremiah 22:15-16; Amos 5:14-15; and James 2:8-9).

● **God values justice more than acts of piety or worship.** God prizes truth, honesty, and impartiality so much that he refuses our "religious" deeds when we treat each other unjustly (Proverbs 21:2-3; Isaiah 1:11-17; Amos 5:21-24; Micah 6:6-8; and Matthew 23:23-24).

- **God wants justice to characterize individuals, groups, and social institutions.** Although we should treat each other fairly on a personal level, that isn't enough. We should also work for just laws and oppose unjust practices such as discrimination, oppression, and exploitation (Amos 2:6-7a; Micah 2:1-3; 3:1-3; Ephesians 6:9; and James 2:1-4).

- **Legal justice demands that everyone follow the law.** Leaders may not disregard the law to favor themselves or others. No one should try to subvert the law through lies or bribes; instead, everyone should seek to create a legal system that reflects God's standard of justice (2 Samuel 23:2-4; Psalm 72:1-4, 12-14; and Amos 5:12-15).

- **Social justice is more important than legal justice.** Even a "legal" act is unjust when it denies someone fair treatment. For example, it's unjust to take advantage of the poor or to show favoritism to the rich even if the law allows us to do so (Deuteronomy 24:17; Amos 5:11-12; 8:4-7; Luke 11:42; Colossians 4:1; and James 1:27).

- **Victims of injustice can cry out to God for help.** God is ultimately responsible for maintaining justice, so anyone being treated unjustly can ask him to intervene (Psalms 7:6-11; 26:1-3; 119:153-159; Hebrews 5:7; and 1 Peter 4:19).

CORE CHRISTIAN BELIEF OVERVIEW

Here are the twenty-four Core Christian Belief categories that form the backbone of Core Belief Bible Study Series:

The Nature of God	Jesus Christ	The Holy Spirit
Humanity	Evil	Suffering
Creation	The Spiritual Realm	The Bible
Salvation	Spiritual Growth	Personal Character
God's Justice	Sin & Forgiveness	The Last Days
Love	The Church	Worship
Authority	Prayer	Family
Service	Relationships	Sharing Faith

Look for Group's Core Belief Bible Study Series books in these other Core Christian Beliefs!

Bible Study Series
for senior high

Think for a moment about your young people. When your students walk out of your youth program after they graduate from junior high or high school, what do you want them to know? What foundation do you want them to have so they can make wise choices?

You probably want them to know the essentials of the Christian faith. You want them to base everything they do on the foundational truths of Christianity. Are you meeting this goal?

If you have any doubt that your kids will walk into adulthood knowing and living by the tenets of the Christian faith, then you've picked up the right book. All the books in Group's Core Belief Bible Study Series encourage young people to discover the essentials of Christianity and to put those essentials into practice. Let us explain...

What Is Group's Core Belief Bible Study Series?

Group's Core Belief Bible Study Series is a biblically in-depth study series for junior high and senior high teenagers. This Bible study series utilizes four defining commitments to create each study. These "plumb lines" provide structure and continuity for every activity, study, project, and discussion. They are:

● **A Commitment to Biblical Depth**—Core Belief Bible Study Series is founded on the belief that kids not only *can* understand the deeper truths of the Bible but also *want* to understand them. Therefore, the activities and studies in this series strive to explain the "why" behind every truth we explore. That way, kids learn principles, not just rules.

● **A Commitment to Relevance**—Most kids aren't interested in abstract theories or doctrines about the universe. They want to know how to live successfully right now, today, in the heat of problems they can't ignore. Because of this, each study connects a real-life need with biblical principles that speak directly to that need. This study series finally bridges the gap between Bible truths and the real-world issues kids face.

● **A Commitment to Variety**—Today's young people have been raised in a sound bite world. They demand variety. For that reason, no two meetings in this study series are shaped exactly the same.

● **A Commitment to Active and Interactive Learning**—Active learning is learning by doing. Interactive learning simply takes active learning a step further by having kids teach each other what they've learned. It's a process that helps kids internalize and remember their discoveries.

For a more detailed description of these concepts, see the section titled "Why Active and Interactive Learning Works With Teenagers" beginning on page 57.

So how can you accomplish all this in a set of four easy-to-lead Bible studies? By weaving together various "power" elements to produce a fun experience that leaves kids challenged and encouraged.

THE ISSUE: Relationships

Betrayed!

B E T R A Y E D

HELPING KIDS DEAL WITH REJECTION FROM THE PEOPLE THEY LOVE

by Jennifer Carrell

THE POINT:

God is love.

■ Betrayal has very little shock value for this generation. It's as commonplace as compact discs and mosh pits. For many kids today, betrayal characterizes their parents' wedding vows. It's part of their curriculum at school; it defines the headlines and evening news. Betrayal is not only accepted—it's expected. ■ At the heart of such acceptance lies the belief that nothing is absolute. No vow, no law, no promise can be trusted. Relationships are betrayed at the earliest convenience. Repeatedly, kids see that something called "love" lasts just as long as it's ... permanence. But deep inside, they hunger to see a ...

The Study
AT A GLANCE

SECTION	MINUTES	WHAT STUDENTS WILL DO	SUPPLIES
Discussion Starter	up to 5	JUMP-START—Identify some of the most common themes in today's movies.	Newsprint, marker
Investigation of Betrayal	12 to 15	REALITY CHECK—Form groups to compare anonymous, real-life stories of betrayal with experiences in their own lives.	"Profiles of Betrayal" handouts (p. 20), highlighter pens, newsprint, marker, tape
	3 to 5	WHO BETRAYED WHOM?—Guess the identities of the people profiled in the handouts.	Paper, tape, pen
Investigation of True Love	15 to 18	SOURCE WORK—Study and discuss God's definition of perfect love.	Bibles, newsprint, marker
	5 to 7	LOVE MESSAGES—Create unique ways to send a "message of love" to the victims of betrayal they've been studying.	Newsprint, markers, tape
Personal Application	10 to 15	SYMBOLIC LOVE—Give a partner a personal symbol of perfect love.	Paper lunch sack, pens, scissors, paper, catalogs

notes:

Betrayed! 16
Permission to photocopy this page from Group's Core Belief Bible Study Series granted for local church use.
Copyright © Group Publishing, Inc., Box 481, Loveland, CO 80539.

● **A Relevant Topic**—More than ever before, kids live in the now. What matters to them and what attracts their hearts is what's happening in their world at this moment. For this reason, every Core Belief Bible Study focuses on a particular hot topic that kids care about.

● **A Core Christian Belief**—Group's Core Belief Bible Study Series organizes the wealth of Christian truth and experience into twenty-four Core Christian Belief categories. These twenty-four headings act as umbrellas for a collection of detailed beliefs that define Christianity and set it apart from the world and every other religion. Each book in this series features one Core Christian Belief with lessons suited for junior high or senior high students.

"But," you ask, "won't my kids be bored talking about all these spiritual beliefs?" No way! As a youth leader, you know the value of using hot topics to connect with young people. Ultimately teenagers talk about issues because they're searching for meaning in their lives. They want to find the one equation that will make sense of all the confusing events happening around them. Each Core Belief Bible Study answers that need by connecting a hot topic with a powerful Christian principle. Kids walk away from the study with something more solid than just the shifting ebb and flow of their own opinions. They walk away with a deeper understanding of their Christian faith.

● **The Point**—This simple statement is designed to be the intersection between the Core Christian Belief and the hot topic. Everything in the study ultimately focuses on The Point so that kids study it and allow it time to sink into their hearts.

● **The Study at a Glance**—A quick look at this chart will tell you what kids will do, how long it will take them to do it, and what supplies you'll need to get it done.

• The Bible Connection—This is the power base of each study. Whether it's just one verse or several chapters, The Bible Connection provides the vital link between kids' minds and their hearts. The content of each Core Belief Bible Study reflects the belief that the true power of God—the power to expose, heal, and change kids' lives—is contained in his Word.

THE POINT OF *BETRAYED!*:

God is love.

THE BIBLE CONNECTION

1 JOHN 4:7-21   The Apostle John explains the nature and definition of perfect love.

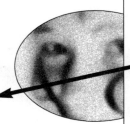

In this study, kids will compare the imperfect love defined in real-life stories of betrayal to God's definition of perfect love.

By making this comparison, kids can discover that God is love and therefore incapable of betraying them. Then they'll be able to recognize the incredible opportunity God offers to experience the only relationship worthy of their absolute trust.

Explore the verses in The Bible Connect~~ion~~ mation in the Depthfinder boxes throughou~~t~~ understanding of how these Scriptures con~~~~

LEADER
TIP
for The Study

THE STUDY

DISCUSSION STARTER ▼

Jump-Start (up to 5 minutes) As kids arrive, ask them to thi~~nk~~ common themes in movies, books, TV sho~~ws~~ have kids each contribute ideas for a mas~~ter~~ two other kids in the room and sharing ~~their~~ sider providing copies of People maga~~zine t~~ what's currently showing on televisi~~on, or at~~ their suggestions, write their respo~~nses on ne~~ **come up with a lot of great ide~~as~~. Even th~~ ~~ent, look through this list an~~d~~ try to disc~~over~~ ments most of these theme~~s~~ have in com~~mon.~~

After kids make several s~~u~~ggestions, menti~~on~~ responses are connected w~~ith~~ the idea of bet~~rayal.~~

● **Why do you think ~~b~~etrayal is such a ~~~~**

Betrayed! **17**

LEADER
TIP
for The Study

Because this topic can be so powerful and relevant to kids' lives, your group members may be tempted to get caught up in issues and lose sight of the deeper biblical principle found in The Point. Help your kids grasp The Point by guiding kids to focus on the biblical investigation and discussing how God's truth connects with reality in their lives.

DEPTH FINDER   UNDERSTANDING INTEGRITY

Your students may not be entirely familiar with the meaning of integrity, especially as it might apply to God's character in the Trinity. Use these definitions (taken from Webster's II New Riverside Dictionary) and other information to help you guide kids toward a better understanding of how God maintains integrity through the three expressions of the Trinity.

Integrity: 1. Firm adherence to a code or standard of values. 2. The state of being unimpaired. 3. The quality or condition of being undivided.

Synonyms for integrity include probity, completeness, wholeness, soundness, and perfection.

Our word "integrity" comes from the Latin word *integritas,* which means soundness. *Integritas* is also the root of the word "integer," which means "whole or complete," as in a "whole" number.

The Hebrew word that's often translated "integrity" (for example, in Psalm 25:21 [NIV]) is *tam.* It means whole, perfect, sincere, and honest.

CREATIVE GOD-EXPLORATION ▼

Top Hats (18 to 20 minutes) Form three groups, with each trio member from the previous activity going to a different group. Give each group Bibles, paper, and pens, and assign each group a different hat God wears: Father, Son, or Holy Spirit.

~~their goal is to write one list describing what God does in the~~

• Depthfinder Boxes— These informative sidelights located throughout each study add insight into a particular passage, word, historical fact, or Christian doctrine. Depthfinder boxes also provide insight into teen culture, adolescent development, current events, and philosophy.

• Leader Tips— These handy information boxes coach you through the study, offering helpful suggestions on everything from altering activities for different-sized groups to streamlining discussions to using effective discipline techniques.

holy Profiles

Your assigned Bible passage describes how a particular person or group responded when confronted with God's holiness. Use the information in your passage to help your group discuss the questions below. Then use your flashlights to teach the other two groups what you discover.

◼ Based on your passage, what does holiness look like?

◼ What does holiness sound like?

◼ When people see God's holiness, how does it affect them?

◼ How is this response to God's holiness like humility?

◼ Based on your passage, how would you describe humility?

◼ Why is humility an appropriate human response to God's holiness?

◼ Based on what you see in your passage, do you think you are a humble person? Why or why not?

◼ What's one way you could develop humility in your life this week?

• Handouts—Most Core Belief Bible Studies include photocopiable handouts to use with your group. Handouts might take the form of a fun game, a lively discussion starter, or a challenging study page for kids to take home—anything to make your study more meaningful and effective.

Permission to photocopy this handout from Group's Core Belief Bible Study Series granted for local church use.
Copyright © Group Publishing, Inc., Box 481, Loveland, CO 80539.

The Last Word on Core Belief Bible Studies

Soon after you begin to use Group's Core Belief Bible Study Series, you'll see signs of real growth in your group members. Your kids will gain a deeper understanding of the Bible and of their own Christian faith. They'll see more clearly how a relationship with Jesus affects their daily lives. And they'll grow closer to God.

But that's not all. You'll also see kids grow closer to one another.

That's because this series is founded on the principle that Christian faith grows best in the context of relationship. Each study uses a variety of interactive pairs and small groups and always includes discussion questions that promote deeper relationships. The friendships kids will build through this study series will enable them to grow *together* toward a deeper relationship with God.

HeLPiNG KiDs DiSCERN RiGHT FrOM WRoNG

by Michael D. Warden

ABSOLUTE TRUTH

THE POINT:

God's holiness sets the standard for right and wrong.

■ **IS TRUTH DEAD?** The San Francisco Chronicle surveyed Bay-area junior highers to discover their beliefs about sex. The newspaper found that two-thirds of the boys and almost half of the girls believe it's OK for a man to force sex on a woman—if the couple has been dating for at least six months. ■ **IS TRUTH DEAD?** In the 1940s, less than a quarter of college students admitted (anonymously) to cheating in high school. Today three-quarters openly admit to cheating. ■ **IS TRUTH DEAD?** When a Harvard student was asked to remove a Confederate flag that she had draped from her fourth-floor dormitory window, she refused, responding, "If they talk about diversity, they're gonna get it. If they talk about tolerance, they better be ready to have it." ■ **IS TRUTH DEAD?** What would your students say? ■ This study takes kids on a journey into a world devoid of absolutes to help young people discover the chaos that erupts whenever right and wrong are ignored. Through this experience, kids can learn that God's holiness sets the one standard for godly behavior in all our lives.

The Study
AT A GLANCE

SECTION	MINUTES	WHAT STUDENTS WILL DO	SUPPLIES
Relational Time	up to 5	PERSONAL TABOO—Discuss choices or behaviors that they believe are always wrong.	Bible, newsprint
Learning Game	35 to 40	ABSOLUTE CONFUSION—Create scenarios for other teams to act out while the "laws of reality" change.	Newsprint, tape, markers
Debriefing	5 to 10	TWO FOR THE TRUTH—Work with partners to create lists of truths that they derive from the previous activity.	Bibles with concordances, newsprint, markers, tape, pencils, "Absolute Truth" handouts (p. 23)
Prayer Experience	5 to 10	UNITY IN TRUTH—Pray that the truths they discovered will become part of the foundation of their lives.	

notes:

Permission to photocopy this page from Group's Core Belief Bible Study Series granted for local church use.
Copyright © Group Publishing, Inc., P.O. Box 481, Loveland, CO 80539.

THE POINT OF *ABSOLUTE TRUTH:*

God's holiness sets the standard for right and wrong.

THE BIBLE CONNECTION	
2 CORINTHIANS 7:1	Paul encourages us to live holy lives out of respect for God.
1 PETER 1:13-16	Peter instructs us to be holy because God is holy.

I n this study, kids will form teams to accomplish tasks while the rules that govern their actions and their environment constantly change.

   Through this experience, kids can discover the chaos that arises any time people deny the existence of absolute truth. Kids can also learn several truths that they can apply to their lives.

   Explore the verses in The Bible Connection; then examine the information in the Depthfinder boxes throughout the study to gain a deeper understanding of how these Scriptures connect with your young people.

LEADER TIP
for The Study
Whenever groups discuss a list of questions, write the list on newsprint, and tape it to a wall so groups can answer the questions at their own pace.

THE STUDY

RELATIONAL TIME ▼

Personal Taboo (up to 5 minutes) Have kids form pairs, and give each pair a two-by-two-foot sheet of newsprint to stand on. Once each pair is standing on its newsprint square, say: **Let's discover whether you and your partner see eye to eye on some important issues of right and wrong. I'm going to call out a series of statements. If *both* you and your partner absolutely agree or absolutely disagree with the statement**

I call out, do nothing. But if *one* of you disagrees even a little with the statement, he or she must tear off half of the newsprint you're standing on together. Then you must try to stand together on the newsprint that remains.

Once kids understand the instructions, read the statements below. Allow time after reading each statement for pairs to agree or disagree and to rip their newsprint squares if necessary. Call out the following statements one at a time.

● **Abortion is murder.**

DEPTHFINDER
HELPING KIDS UNDERSTAND RIGHT FROM WRONG

Your kids live in a world without moral absolutes. So how can you enter their world and make an impact with truth? Try these tactics:

1. **Examine moral relativism with your kids.** You can begin by leading this study with your kids. But be warned! Even when you point out that believing in moral relativism means no one can ever be wrong, your kids may argue that society at large can determine what's right and wrong for the people within it. Your kids might say, "Murder is wrong in this country because most people in our society believe it's wrong. And, in the same way, abortion is legal because the majority of people think it's OK."

If kids raise this argument, ask them about Nazism, Hitler, and the Holocaust. Hitler's Germany believed it was "right" to extinguish the Jews from the face of the earth. In a relativistic world, the Nazis wouldn't be condemned for this belief, and yet they were. Why? Was their society "wrong"? And if a society can be wrong, how can I trust that my society is right when it says abortion is OK?

2. **Focus kids on the need for trust in relationships.** In a world without absolutes, nothing and no one can be trusted absolutely. Betrayal—not commitment—is the norm for relationships. For example, the research of Christian pollster George Barna showed that four out of five kids rank "having one marriage partner for life" as "very desirable." But in a world without moral absolutes, what happens if the marriage is no longer "right for me"? In that case, staying in the marriage would become the "wrong" thing to do, regardless of my partner's desires.

3. **Encourage kids toward a closer personal relationship with Jesus.** Because Jesus is the Truth, encourage kids to get to know him better. The more time they spend with him and in his Word, the more willing they'll become to accept Christ's holiness as the standard for right and wrong.

4. **Point kids to God's "bottom line."** Today's kids know they'll have to sacrifice a great deal to fix the problems they've inherited from their elders: drugs, war, poverty, the national debt, Social Security shortfall, welfare fraud, educational failures, pollution—the list goes on. When confronted with these issues, they'll typically respond with gritty realism. "Just tell us how much it's going to cost," they say. And then they're willing to pay it.

That mind-set can also help them understand the unchangeable nature of moral absolutes. Whether we like it or not, God is God, and he has set up certain moral absolutes that cannot be circumvented or ignored, any more than gravity can be suspended or death can be permanently denied. God's moral absolutes are a reality of life on earth, and we have to learn to deal with them on a daily basis. Your kids will understand language like that. So don't be skittish about telling them God's bottom line. It's the language of the real world.

● It would be good to have a national death penalty for serious criminals.

● It isn't necessarily wrong for a couple to live together before they're married.

● Sex before marriage is always wrong.

● A parent should be allowed to discipline a child by striking the child on the bottom.

● There is more than one path to eternal life.

● One person's idea of truth may not be the same as another person's. There is no such thing as absolute truth.

After reading all the statements and allowing kids to respond, have pairs discuss these questions:

● Was this experience difficult? Why or why not?

● How was standing together on the newsprint similar to sharing common beliefs about right and wrong?

● What happened as the newsprint got smaller?

● How is that similar to losing "common ground" when your beliefs about right and wrong change?

● Do you think there is an absolute right or wrong for any of the issues we mentioned? Why or why not?

● How can we know that some action or attitude is always wrong? Who has the authority to make that decision?

Ask for a volunteer to read aloud 2 Corinthians 7:1 to the group. Then ask for a different volunteer to read 1 Peter 1:13-16 aloud. Then have pairs discuss the following:

● What do these Scriptures say about how we should act? about why we should act that way?

Say: **Many people today believe that deciding right from wrong is a personal issue. And to a degree, that's a healthy perspective. After all, it's not up to me to tell you whether you should wear purple pants or change your name to Englebert Jones. But there are some actions and attitudes in life that are always wrong. How do I know? Because <u>God's holiness sets the standard for right and wrong.</u> By examining what God says is holy or profane, I can tell whether something is right or wrong for me—and for everyone else.**

LEARNING GAME ▼

Absolute Confusion

(35 to 40 minutes)

Say: **We all believe in absolute truth whether we admit it or not. How do I know? Because without absolute truth, life would be nothing but chaos. Let's do a fun experiment to demonstrate that we all believe in absolute truth.**

Have kids form teams of four to six. Then set out chairs, newsprint, markers, and tape. Say: **In a moment, teams are going to take turns building altars to God. When it's your team's turn, the rest of the class will tell your team members how they are related to each other and where the altar construction will take place. For**

DEPTHFINDER — UNDERSTANDING THE CULTURE OF RELATIVISM

The popular teenage belief that you can build your own reality—and, therefore, define your own truth—has created for your young people an entire culture of relativism. Relativism says, in essence, "If it works for you, it must be good. I have no right to judge your choices. I can only make choices for myself." Nobody has to believe the same things, do the same things, or think the same way. You can be the master of your own fate because no one can know what's right (or wrong) for you better than you do.

This may all sound reasonable and even respectful on the surface, but such a relativistic belief has one fatal flaw: Without an external, self-existent standard of absolute truth, no one's actions can ever be truly deemed "wrong" or even "inappropriate." If I feel like loving you today, that's OK. But if I get up tomorrow and decide to kill you, that's got to be OK, too. After all, with no absolute standard of right and wrong, who can judge me?

That fatal flaw in relativistic thought offers the strongest argument for God's holy standard of absolute truth. Today's young people want beliefs that'll work for them in the real world every day. Ultimately, relativism *doesn't* work. It's neither practical nor true. When your kids see that, it won't be long before they abandon their relativistic beliefs for something better—God's absolute truth.

instance, the class might say, "You're all sailors on a life raft in the Pacific Ocean." Then your team must construct an altar as if you're sailors stuck on a life raft.

But that's not all. As each team takes its turn, I'll change the "laws of reality" by calling out new right-and-wrong beliefs that teams also must act out. For example, if I say, "Cheating is good," then all the team members must try to cheat each other as they work on building their altar.

Once teams understand the instructions, choose a team to go first. Have the rest of the class decide how the team members should be related and where the action should take place. For example, team members could be members of the Mafia on a drug plane, or they could be family members who work together as trapeze artists in a circus. Allow the team to work for two minutes, using the supplies you set out to create an altar. When time is up, stop the action, and allow another team to come up and construct a new altar. Once again, have the class call out a location and decide how all the team members are related. Continue until all the teams have had a chance to work.

As each team works on its altar, change the "laws of reality" by calling out one of the statements below. Call out a new statement every thirty seconds or so. It's OK if you repeat some laws more than once. Here are the laws:

- **No one else matters except you.**
- **Destroying trees or wildlife is a sin worthy of death.**
- **Hate makes you powerful.**
- **You are all gods.**
- **The person who's wearing the most red is a god.**
- **Cheating is good.**
- **You can never tell another person what to do.**

Two for the Truth

(5 to 10 minutes)

After all the teams have finished, have kids gather together on the floor around the altar created by the last team. Have kids form pairs, and give each pair a pencil and an "Absolute Truth" handout (p. 23). Make sure each pair has access to a Bible with a good concordance. Say: **Go through the handout with your partner. Use a Bible and a concordance to help you discover at least five absolute truths that counter many of the false beliefs we heard in the last activity.**

As pairs work, tape a sheet of newsprint to a wall, and set out several markers. As pairs finish, have them write on the newsprint each of the truths they discovered, along with the Bible passages they used to validate each truth.

Say: **Who would've thought there were so many absolute truths in life? By listening to many of the voices in the world, it would be easy to believe there was no such thing as absolute truth at all. But because we know God, we know better. <u>God's holiness sets the standard for right and wrong.</u>** He defines absolute truth and shows us how to live as we should.

"AS OBEDIENT do not children, conform to the EVIL desires you had when you lived in ignorance. BUT JUST AS HE WHO CALLED YOU IS HOLY, SO BE HOLY IN ALL YOU DO." —1 Peter 1:14-15

Unity in Truth

(5 to 10 minutes)

Say: **Absolute truth can be hard to swallow because sometimes we all want to do our own thing in our own way. But absolute truth is kind of like God's "bottom line." There's no way around it. We have to humble ourselves and recognize that in many situations, we don't define what's right and wrong. God's holiness sets that standard for us.**

Have each student find a new partner to discuss these questions:

● **Are you willing to submit to God's absolute truth as it's explained in Scripture? Why or why not?**

● **What's one absolute truth that your partner demonstrates well?**

● **What's one truth you want to learn to submit to better in your own life?**

Have pairs kneel together and pray for each other. Have pairs pray that God will grant them the humility to submit to his truth and that they'll let his truth guide their choices in daily life.

(Portions of this study are adapted from "Teaching Black-and-White Truths to Gray-Minded Kids," Michael Warden, GROUP Magazine, September/October 1995.)

ABSOLUTE TRUTH

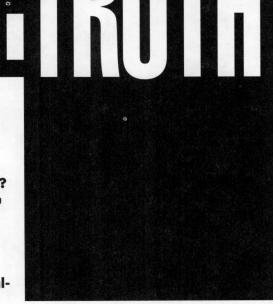

DiSCUSs ThESe QuESTiONs:

● What's your reaction to the altar-building activity?

● Was it difficult trying to build an altar while the "laws of reality" kept changing? Why or why not? How did that make you feel?

● How is that experience similar to what it would be like to follow God in a world with no absolutes?

● What would the world be like if there really were no such thing as absolute truth?

● What's one absolute truth that you believe and try to live out in your life?

● How do you know your belief really is an absolute truth and not just your own opinion?

We all have opinions about things, but we can tell whether an opinion is absolute truth by looking in the Bible. God's Word describes for us God's holy character. And God's holiness sets the standard for right and wrong in our lives.

Examine the list of false beliefs you encountered in the altar-building activity. Then use a Bible and a concordance to find one or more absolute truths in Scripture that nullify each false belief. Your leader will tell you how many absolute truths you must find.

Here are the false beliefs you heard in the altar-building activity:

● No one else matters except you.
● Destroying trees or wildlife is a sin worthy of death.
● Hate makes you powerful.
● You are all gods.
● The person who's wearing the most red is a god.
● Cheating is good.
● You can never tell another person what to do.

iN ThIS SpACE, wrITe ThE ScRiPTURe PaSSAGEs AND AbSoLUTe TrUTHs YOU DiSCOVER:

Permission to photocopy this handout from Group's Core Belief Bible Study Series granted for local church use.
Copyright © Group Publishing, Inc., P.O. Box 481, Loveland, CO 80539.

"That's Not Fair!"

Helping Kids Trust in God's Justice

by Tim and Jacqui Baker

THE POINT:

God's justice will never fail you.

■ AIDS. Divorce. The national debt. Abusive parents. Low wages. Useless education. Alcohol abuse. Environmental destruction. Bankrupt social security. Air pollution. Governmental corruption. Homelessness. Gangs. Global warming. School violence. Drive-by shootings. Corporate layoffs. Abusive clergy. Drug addiction. Suicide. ■ Life isn't fair. And your kids know it. You can hear it whenever they talk about the future or look into the past. You can see it in their faces every time another friend's parents opt for divorce or another government official resigns in a cloud of suspicion. ■ It's a confusing world of wrong endings and unfair choices. Your kids are crying out for someone to help them understand why life seems anything but fair. ■ Are you listening? ■ This study explores the difference between fairness and justice and exposes young people to a biblical perspective of God's true justice as it relates to their lives and to the world around them.

The Study
AT A GLANCE

SECTION	MINUTES	WHAT STUDENTS WILL DO	SUPPLIES
Relational Exploration	5 to 10	WHAT'S FAIR ABOUT INJUSTICE?—Create human "snapshots" representing their definitions of justice and fairness.	Newsprint, tape, markers
	5 to 10	UNFAIR TREATMENT—Create symbols representing unfair treatment and God's justice.	Pipe cleaners
Digging Deep	20 to 25	VENGEANCE IS WHOSE?—Explore Scriptures related to justice while experiencing unfair treatment.	Bibles, newsprint, paper, markers, pencils
Triad Debrief	5 to 10	STEADY JUSTICE—Compare popular notions of fairness with the Bible's teachings of God's justice.	
Grace Closing	5 to 10	PICTURE OF GRACE—Create a symbol representing God's grace.	Bibles, "Justice vs. Grace" handouts (p. 33), pipe cleaners from "Unfair Treatment"

notes:

Permission to photocopy this page from Group's Core Belief Bible Study Series granted for local church use.
Copyright © Group Publishing, Inc., P.O. Box 481, Loveland, CO 80539.

God's justice will never fail you.

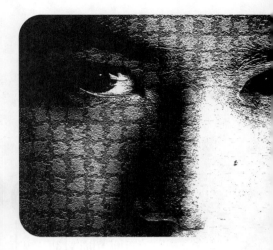

THE BIBLE CONNECTION

EZEKIEL 34:16-24	God will judge between the "sheep, rams, and goats."
HEBREWS 10:30-31	Paul reminds God's suffering people to persevere because God will ultimately judge everyone.
REVELATION 20:11-15	John gives a vivid account of how God's justice will ultimately be revealed.

I n this study, kids will experience how it feels to be treated unfairly and will search through three Scriptures to discover how God's justice ultimately prevails.

By contrasting God's justice with our culture's sense of fairness, your students will see how reliable and true God's justice really is—and how popular notions of fairness often don't measure up to God's truth.

Explore the verses in The Bible Connection; then examine the information in the Depthfinder boxes throughout the study to gain a deeper understanding of how these Scriptures connect with your young people.

LEADER TIP for The Study

Whenever groups discuss a list of questions, write the list on newsprint, and tape it to a wall so groups can discuss the questions at their own pace.

BEFORE THE STUDY

For the "What's Fair About Injustice?" activity, tape up a sheet of newsprint at each end of the meeting room. On one sheet, write "Justice"; on the other, write "Fairness."

THE STUDY

RELATIONAL EXPLORATION ▼

LEADER TIP

for What's Fair About Injustice?

To help kids come up with good definitions for "fairness" and "justice," provide dictionaries that kids can use to look up words they're unsure about.

What's Fair About Injustice? (5 to 10 minutes)

As kids arrive, distribute markers, and direct kids to the two pieces of newsprint you taped up before the study. Have kids write their own definitions to each of these words on the appropriate sheet of newsprint. Once kids have written their definitions, have kids form trios to discuss these questions:

- **What's your favorite definition for fairness? for justice?**
- **What do you think is the main difference between justice and fairness?**
- **Would you say that God is fair or just? Explain.**

Say: **Understanding the difference between what's just and what's fair can be confusing. Maybe the difference can be seen best as a picture. In a moment, I'm going to ask you to demonstrate how you define justice and fairness by creating a group "snapshot."**

Assign each trio one of these words: justice or fairness. Give each trio three minutes to form itself into a group snapshot that demonstrates the group's favorite definition of the assigned word.

After three minutes, create a group "photo album" by asking each group to unveil its snapshot and explain its meaning. Once the entire photo album has been shown, ask:

- **How do you feel when you're treated unfairly?**
- **Where is God when you're being treated unfairly?**
- **What do you think God's response is when you're being treated unfairly?**
- **Regardless of how unfair a situation may feel, do you believe that God's justice will never fail you? Why or why not?**

Unfair Treatment (5 to 10 minutes)

Say: **Everyone in this room has been treated unfairly at one time or another. Because we know that life is unfair at times, it can be easy for us to say that God is unfair. After all, not all of us are born with the same talents or abilities. And we certainly don't all have the same parents. But that doesn't mean God is unjust or doesn't treat us as well as we deserve. When we learn that our idea of fairness and the Bible's idea of God's justice aren't the same, we can begin to believe that no matter how unfair life seems to be, God's justice will never fail us. Let's explore the difference between God's justice and our culture's notion of fairness.**

Why?

Give each person a pipe cleaner; then have each person come up with an ending to the statement, "I was treated unfairly when…" Give

DEPTH FINDER

UNDERSTANDING THESE KIDS

Young people think about justice more than we might imagine. For example, do you ever wonder what young people think about the United States' legal system? Well, The Gallup Youth Survey took a poll to find out ("Justice Not So Blind in the U.S.," Youthviews newsletter, May 1995). Here's a sampling of what they found:

Sixty-four percent of teenagers say they agree with the statement, "The laws usually do more to give rights to criminals than to protect their victims."

Sixty-three percent of teenagers say they agree with the statement, "Rich people almost never go to jail, because they can hire smart lawyers."

Only 52 percent of teenagers agree that "the U.S. probably has the fairest legal system in the world."

These statistics raise some troubling questions for Christian youth leaders. For example, if our kids believe that U.S. laws protect criminals more than the innocent, how do they feel about God's justice?

[handwritten: Discuss these 3 statements of our justice system.]

[handwritten: B]

kids one minute to think, and then have them mold their pipe cleaners into shapes that represent their answers.

After kids have finished, have them form pairs and explain their pipe cleaner shapes to their partners. Then ask kids to come up with an ending to the statement, "One way God's justice could come through for me in that situation is…" *[handwritten: 4]* Give kids one minute to think, and then have them mold their pipe cleaners into shapes that represent their answers.

After kids have finished, have them explain their new pipe cleaner shapes to their partners. Then have pairs discuss these questions:

● **Through this activity, can you see how God's justice will never fail you? Why or why not?**

● **How was reshaping the pipe cleaner like the way God might reshape circumstances in your life so that justice prevails?**

✱ **If God's justice never fails us, how can we explain the many unfair and unjust situations we see every day?**

● **Since God's justice never fails us, how should we react to unfair treatment in our lives?**

Say: **When we see injustice in the world—or in our own lives—it sometimes is hard to believe that God is still in control or that he loves us at all. But we must remember that no unjust situation ever goes uncorrected. God's justice will never fail us, though the manner and timing of his justice are totally in his control. He doesn't necessarily take action when *we want;* he takes action when *it's best.***

DIGGING DEEP ▼

Vengeance Is Whose?

(20 to 25 minutes)

Say: **Let's take a look at how others have dealt with unfair situations, and let's see how God has intervened. That way, we can get a clearer understanding of how**

LEADER TIP

for Vengeance Is Whose? (Group 1)

If other groups will be meeting in the same building during the study, let them know about your activity, and give your students boundaries in order to avoid disturbing other groups.

LEADER TIP

for Vengeance Is Whose?

The exercises in this activity will not only help your kids understand their assigned Scripture passages, but will also cause some of your kids to feel that they're being treated unfairly. That's OK. If kids say the activity is unfair, gently acknowledge their complaint, but don't change the activity. The tension kids feel as they go through this activity will help lead them to a greater understanding of God's justice during the debriefing section in the next activity.

POINT ☞ **God's justice will never fail us.**

Have the kids form three groups. Assign each group one of these Scriptures: Ezekiel 34:16-24; Hebrews 10:30-31; and Revelation 20:11-15. Within their groups, have kids sum up the main idea in the Scripture. Then assign groups the corresponding exploratory exercises below.

Group 1—Ezekiel 34:16-24

Ask this group to go throughout the building, looking for objects that represent different verses in the Scripture. Tell the members of this group that they need to be ready to explain in detail how each object they selected represents one of the verses in the Scripture.

Group 2—Hebrews 10:30-31

Give this group newsprint and markers, and instruct group members to create a group drawing using only their feet to hold the markers. Tell group members to draw a picture that represents the true meaning of their assigned Scripture. Once their drawing is complete, have a representative from the group explain the drawing's meaning to the rest of the class.

Group 3—Revelation 20:11-15

Distribute paper and pencils, and tell this group that it has five minutes to accomplish its task. First, group members must create a final-judgment scene. Next, they must create a three-page script detailing what they think God's final judgment on the world will look like based on the one described in the passage. Finally, they must construct a "lake of fire." Time the group to be sure it doesn't go beyond its five-minute limit.

When time is up, have groups present their assignments to the rest of the class.

"Therefore this is what the Sovereign Lord says to them: See, I myself will judge between the fat sheep and the lean sheep. Because you shove with flank and shoulder, butting all the weak sheep with your horns until you have driven them away, I will save my flock, and they will no longer be plundered. I will judge between one sheep and another."

—Ezekiel 34:20-22

DEPTHFINDER UNDERSTANDING FAIRNESS

Fairness, equality, compromise—whatever word you choose, it's clear that our society views justice and fairness differently from how God does. Your kids are exposed to a whole spectrum of ideas concerning the true nature of justice, from ideas which support that all "justice" is simply veiled revenge to ideas which support that no matter how you're treated, you always deserve it. And in between those extremes lies a generation of young people caught in the middle, asking, "Why is life so unfair?"

When the Bible speaks about fairness, it usually refers to the way we treat others. It speaks specifically about the fair treatment of slaves (see Colossians 4:1) and about the fair judgment of others (see Proverbs 29:14).

But how do you reconcile the "real world" that treats kids unfairly with the Creator's command that everyone be treated with justice? By directing kids to this truth: God judges fairly even though the world has no real idea what true justice is.

By helping kids understand this truth, you'll also be teaching them that God loves them more than life itself and that his justice will never fail them.

TRIAD DEBRIEF ▼

Steady Justice (5 to 10 minutes)
After all three groups have presented their finished assignments, have kids form trios composed of one member from each of the three groups. Have trios discuss these questions:

● **Was any group treated unfairly? Explain.**

● **Is it right to say that one group is being treated unfairly just because it's being treated differently from another group? Why or why not?**

● **How can you ever really gauge what is fair or what isn't fair?**

● **Is there an unchanging standard for what is fair? Why or why not?**

Say: **Apart from God and the Bible, determining what's fair or isn't fair often depends on circumstances and the attitudes of the people involved. For example, at one time in our history, some people believed that Jews were the cause of many of the world's problems. These people felt that it was unfair for Jews to be allowed to live. As a result, millions of Jews were slaughtered. That may not seem fair to us now, but at the time, almost an entire nation thought it was the right thing to do.**

God's justice isn't like that. It's unchanging, and <u>it will never fail you.</u> Even if someone treats you poorly for the most ridiculous reason, in the end, God will bring about justice in your life.

Have kids share with their trio members the main idea of the Bible passage they studied in their previous groups. Then have trios discuss these questions:

● **From what you've seen, how is society's idea of fairness different from God's justice?**

● **What's one area of your life in which you need God's justice to act on your behalf?**

Once kids have shared, have them pray together for God's justice to be established in one another's lives. After the prayer, have kids tell each of their trio members one way they see God's justice at work in his or her life—for example, "I can see how God's justice is working in your life because you have a new job with a boss who treats you better than the last one."

GRACE CLOSING ▼

LEADER TIP for Picture of Grace

If you have more than fifteen kids, have them form two groups for this closing activity to allow everyone time to share.

Picture of Grace (5 to 10 minutes)
Have kids stay in their trios. Say: **Today we've talked about unfair circumstances, and we've looked at God's true and ultimate justice. Let's close by taking a look at the other side of justice—God's grace.**

Give each trio a copy of the "Justice vs. Grace" handout (p. 33). Give kids a few minutes to complete their handouts.

After kids have finished, have the group form a circle. Have kids retrieve their pipe cleaners. Then say: **Earlier I asked you to create a pipe cleaner shape that represented something unfair in your life. Now I'd like you to take that same pipe cleaner and create a symbol that represents God's grace toward us all.**

After kids have finished, have them take turns explaining their symbols to the group and then placing their symbols in the center of the circle. After everyone has shared, close with prayer, thanking God for his incredible, undeserved grace toward us.

Justice vs. Grace

Justice and grace ... hmm... Those are difficult concepts to understand. Perhaps they're best explained like this:

When you think about the concepts of justice and grace, think of the cross. Because God is a just God, he demands a just payment for our sin. Christ came and died to make that payment. Christ's death on the cross solved the justice issue for God, but it also demonstrated God's grace toward us.

You might say that the cross was the perfect union of justice and grace—God's justice toward sin and God's grace toward us. The Scripture verse below will plunge you right in the middle of this idea.

Read Romans 3:23-25.

Discuss these questions in your group:

● When you read this passage, what comes to mind about God's justice?
● According to this passage, who will receive God's justice?
● According to this passage, who has received God's grace?
● Why would God put his Son to death for you? What does this say to you about God's justice?
● How does knowing that Christ died for you help you understand that **God's justice will never fail you?**

Permission to photocopy this handout from Group's Core Belief Bible Study Series granted for local church use.
Copyright © Group Publishing, Inc., P.O. Box 481, Loveland, CO 80539.

For *His* Eyes Only

Leaving Judgment to God

by Jane Vogel

THE POINT:

Only God has the right to judge people's hearts.

■ "It's all your fault!" ■ "He started it!" ■ "It serves them right!" ■ Kids learn to be expert "finger-pointers" at a young age. As they mature, their finger-pointing may become more subtle, but many teenagers still look outward with judgmental eyes. Teenagers also look outward with idealism, though. So what do they do when the idealism of adolescence runs into the ugly realities of a disease like AIDS? Kids want a way to reconcile the two. The easiest way for them to explain away AIDS—and all kinds suffering—is to find someone to blame. ■ The Bible speaks clearly to the dangers of judging others and speaks clearly to the solution, which is to see ourselves as Christ sees us all: sinners in need of grace. ■ Use this lesson to give kids a new perspective on how they look at others—and themselves.

The Study
AT A GLANCE

SECTION	MINUTES	WHAT STUDENTS WILL DO	SUPPLIES
Introductory Investigation	10 to 15	IMPAIRED JUDGMENT—Try to identify an edible sample using only one sense.	An edible sample as described in the "Before the Study" box (p. 37), paper cups, blindfolds, utensils for tasting the sample, paper, pencils
Group Studies	15 to 20	CONTEMPORARY COMPARISONS—Form groups to explore issues of blaming and judgment.	Bibles, "Group Studies" handout (p. 43), scissors, pencils
Group Presentations	15 to 20	Skits and Sayings—Present skits or sayings to illustrate modern-day parallels to biblical truths.	Bibles, paper, pencils, wastebasket
Application and Affirmation	5 to 10	BLOOD TRANSFUSION—Recognize the power of Jesus' blood to heal all those tainted with sin.	Bibles

notes:

Permission to photocopy this page from Group's Core Belief Bible Study Series granted for local church use.
Copyright © Group Publishing, Inc., P.O. Box 481, Loveland, CO 80539.

THE POINT OF *FOR HIS EYES ONLY:*

Only God has the right to judge people's hearts.

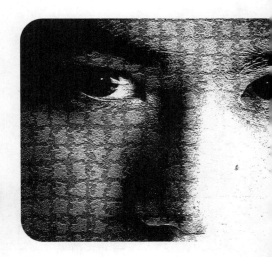

THE BIBLE CONNECTION

MATTHEW 7:1-5	Jesus warns us not to judge others.
JOHN 8:1-11	Jesus refuses to join in a mob's judgment of an adulterous woman.
JOHN 9:1-7	The disciples try to assign blame for a man's blindness.
ROMANS 3:21-26	Paul reminds us that sin is "in our blood" and we all need Jesus' blood.

I n this study, kids will experience firsthand how their judgments are limited by their perceptions; then they'll re-enact biblical events as they relate to modern-day issues about AIDS.

By applying biblical principles to the real-life issues they face, kids can break free from judging others.

Explore the verses in The Bible Connection; then study the information in the Depthfinder boxes throughout the study to gain a deeper understanding of how these Scriptures connect with your young people.

BEFORE THE STUDY

For the "Impaired Judgment" activity, prepare something edible that can't be identified easily by only one sense—banana pudding, red presweetened drink mix, or colorless gelatin, for example. Place the food into four paper cups, and don't forget to provide utensils such as spoons if you need to.

For the "Contemporary Comparisons" activity, make one photocopy of the "Group Studies" handout (p. 43), and cut apart the three sections.

LEADER TIP for The Study

Because this topic can be so powerful and relevant to kids' lives, your group members may be tempted to get caught up in issues and lose sight of the deeper biblical principle found in The Point. Help your kids grasp The Point by guiding them to focus on the biblical investigation and by discussing how God's truth connects with reality in their lives.

THE STUDY

INTRODUCTORY INVESTIGATION ▼

LEADER TIP

for Impaired Judgment

If you know that someone in your group has food allergies, place that person in the smell or sight group.

LEADER TIP

for The Study

Whenever groups discuss a list of questions, write the list on newsprint, and tape it to a wall so groups can discuss the questions at their own pace.

Impaired Judgment (10 to 15 minutes)

As kids arrive, have them form four groups: the taste group, the touch group, the smell group, and the sight group. (Groups can be any size.) Explain that kids are going to try to identify an edible sample by using only one sense. Reassure kids that you're not tricking them into eating anything gross. Then blindfold everyone except the kids in the sight group, and ask kids except those in the smell group to hold their noses.

Give each group a paper cup containing the edible sample, and help the taste group to taste it, the touch group to touch it, and so on. When everyone has "experienced" the sample according to the group he or she is in, hide the paper cups. Then let kids take off their blindfolds. Give each group a pencil and a sheet of paper, and say: **In your group, quietly discuss what you think sample X is. Don't let the other groups hear you. When you reach consensus, write down your conclusion and hand the paper to me. Try to be specific; for example, instead of guessing "soda," you might guess "Diet Dr Pepper."** After groups decide, collect their papers. Most groups will get the answer partially correct—for example, that the sample is an unknown flavor of pudding—but won't get the answer entirely correct.

Next have kids form foursomes, with each foursome including a taster, a toucher, a smeller, and a see-er. Have the members of each foursome pool information to decide what sample X is. Then ask foursomes for their conclusions.

Finally reveal the sample, and have kids discuss the following questions within their foursomes:

● **How did the conclusion in your first group compare with the conclusion in your foursome?**

● **If the two conclusions were different, why were they?**

● **How would this experiment have been different if you had been able to use all your senses?**

● **In your life, have you ever come to a wrong conclusion because you didn't have all the information? If so, what was the situation?**

Say: **If it's this easy to misjudge a sample of** (name of sample X) **that we can at least see or touch or taste or smell, think about how easy it is to misjudge human hearts! Our judgment of others is limited by our perceptions, but God's judgment is not. That's why <u>only God has the right to judge people's hearts.</u>**

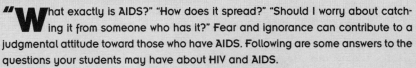

DEPTHFINDER

THE FACTS ABOUT HIV AND AIDS

"What exactly is AIDS?" "How does it spread?" "Should I worry about catching it from someone who has it?" Fear and ignorance can contribute to a judgmental attitude toward those who have AIDS. Following are some answers to the questions your students may have about HIV and AIDS.

● **What do the terms "HIV" and "AIDS" mean?** HIV stands for Human Immunodeficiency Virus. This virus causes AIDS—Acquired Immunodeficiency Syndrome.

● **What happens to someone who contracts HIV/AIDS?** HIV breaks down a person's immune system. The infected person loses the ability to protect himself or herself from germs that most of us can fight. These germs cause cancers, pneumonia, and other infections that lead to death, usually within ten years after HIV is diagnosed. When an HIV-positive person contracts one of these diseases, he or she is considered to have AIDS. At this time, there is no vaccine or cure for HIV or AIDS.

● **How does someone get HIV/AIDS?** HIV is spread through vaginal, anal, or oral sex with someone who is infected with HIV; sharing needles for injecting drugs; or in childbirth or breast-feeding, passed from an infected mother to her child. You can no longer contract HIV/AIDS through blood transfusions—since 1985, all donated blood has been tested for HIV, and today's blood supply is considered safe.

You *cannot* get AIDS from hugs; handshakes; coughs or sneezes; sweat or tears; pets; mosquitoes or other insects; eating food prepared by someone else; or using toilet or shower facilities, eating utensils, drinking fountains, sports equipment, or swimming pools.

● **Who is most likely to get HIV/AIDS?** HIV/AIDS is a disease that does not discriminate. It doesn't matter whether you are male or female, gay or straight or bisexual, old or young. Anyone can get it. But you can keep from contracting the disease if you avoid risky behaviors. (Also see answer to "How does someone get HIV/AIDS?")

Keep in mind that scientists learn more about this disease all the time. Educate yourself through reading and asking questions to maintain current knowledge about HIV/AIDS.

The Centers for Disease Control have a hot line available for questions or statistics about HIV/AIDS. If you have questions, you can call the hot line at 800-342-2437.

(Information compiled from the Centers for Disease Control and the American Red Cross brochures "HIV and AIDS" and "Teenagers and HIV.")

Permission to photocopy this Depthfinder from Group's Core Belief Bible Study Series granted for local church use. Copyright © Group Publishing, Inc., P.O. Box 481, Loveland, CO 80539.

GROUP STUDIES ▼

Contemporary Comparisons

(15 to 20 minutes)

Have kids form three study groups. Give each group one of the sections from the "Group Studies" handout (p. 43), Bibles, and pencils. Say: **Read the instructions on your handout. You have about fifteen minutes to read the Bible passage listed, complete the instructions, and prepare your presentation. You must involve every member of your group in the presentation in**

LEADER TIP

for Contemporary Comparisons

Each study group should have at least three members. If you have fewer than nine kids in your class, have kids form two groups and assign one to do "The Blame Game" and the other "Sticks and Stones." After their presentations, do "Metaphor Makers" all together if time permits.

Study groups of more than eight kids may get unwieldy. If you have a large class, you can form more than three study groups and have more than one group work on each section.

DEPTHFINDER

DOESN'T GOD'S LAW CALL FOR JUDGMENT?

The "teachers of the law and the Pharisees" accusing the adulterous woman in John 8:1-11 weren't really concerned with following Old Testament law. If they had been, they would have brought the woman's partner to be accused as well (see Leviticus 20:10 and Deuteronomy 22:22). Jesus both exposed the accusers' hypocrisy and made the people focus on their own sins before they rushed to judge someone else.

Jesus' mercy in this episode does not mean that he takes sin lightly. Scripture clearly condemns adultery (Exodus 20:14; Deuteronomy 22:22; and Leviticus 20:10), homosexual activity (Leviticus 18:22; 20:13; and Romans 1:24-27), and any form of sexual promiscuity (1 Corinthians 6:9-10 and 1 Timothy 1:8-10). But we should not look today for the kinds of judgments on sin that were so striking in the Old Testament (such as the judgment on Sodom and Gomorrah in Genesis 18:17–19:29). Why? Not because God no longer cares about sin but because he laid the judgment for all sin on his Son, Jesus Christ.

Jesus did not require the adulterous woman's death because he was willing instead to pay with his death.

some way. For example, if you are doing a drama, you can use people as trees or furniture as well as characters.

GROUP PRESENTATIONS ▼

Skits and Sayings
(15 to 20 minutes)

When all the study groups are ready or after fifteen minutes, have Group 1 present its "Blame Game" dramatization. Then have a group member read aloud John 9:1-7. Ask:

● **Why do you think the disciples wanted to know whose fault the man's blindness was?**

● **How do people ask the same sort of blaming questions today when someone suffers?**

● **What do you think Jesus' answer would have been if the blind man had not been born blind but instead had contracted AIDS? Explain.**

● **Do you think AIDS is a consequence of behaviors like promiscuity and intravenous drug use or God's punishment for those actions? Explain.**

Have students open their Bibles and follow along in John 8:1-11 so they can see the parallels as Group 2 presents its drama. When the drama is over, ask:

● **In what ways do people "stone" AIDS patients today?**

Hand out paper and pencils, and have kids privately write one or more feelings, actions, or attitudes they might take toward someone with AIDS—for example, "Well, you only got what you deserved" or "You are totally disgusting." Instruct kids to write their responses to

DEPTHFINDER — DON'T JUDGE ME!

If some of your kids take the injunction not to judge others to mean that no one can judge them—no matter what they do—well, they're not the first. It's always easier to apply Jesus' words to someone other than ourselves, and people have been doing just that since the church began (check out the situation Paul had to address in 1 Corinthians 5:1-5).

Jesus' warning not to judge people is not license for kids to do whatever they want. His words in John 8:11 to the woman caught in adultery apply to us as well: "Go now and leave your life of sin."

someone who contracted AIDS through sexual promiscuity, assuring them that their responses will remain private. Have kids wad their papers up. Explain that attitudes like the ones they wrote may be like "stones" we throw at others. Have kids hold on to their "stones" to look at again later.

● **Why do you think the accusers in the Bible story dropped their stones and walked away?**

● **What would you have done in the same situation?**

● **Why, when adultery is clearly against God's law, didn't Jesus encourage the people to carry out the punishment prescribed in the Old Testament?**

Have a member from Group 3 read aloud Matthew 7:1-5 and all of the group's examples. (Don't worry if the examples aren't all serious. A little humor at this point will be welcome.) Ask:

● **How do you feel about being judged in the same way you judge others?**

● **In what ways does judging others hurt your relationships? Hurt you?**

● **Think about the response to AIDS patients you wrote earlier. How would you feel if someone responded that way to you?**

● **How would you feel if God responded that way to you?**

Say: <u>**Only God has the right to judge people's hearts.**</u> But  way too often, we end up taking the job of judging others.

Have kids offer prayers asking for nonjudgmental hearts. As each person prays, have him or her throw his or her "judgment stone" in the wastebasket as a symbol of getting rid of those judgmental attitudes.

APPLICATION AND AFFIRMATION ▼

Blood Transfusion
(5 to 10 minutes) Have kids form groups of four. In their foursomes, have kids read Romans 3:21-26 and then discuss these questions:

● **How would you respond to someone who says, "God says not to judge, so God must think whatever we do is OK"?**

● **By what one standard does God judge people?** If kids need help with this question, point them to verse 22a ("This righteousness from

LEADER TIP for Blood Transfusion

This passage from Romans 3 offers you a wonderful opportunity to share the gospel message explicitly with any students who have not responded in faith to Jesus Christ. Don't be afraid to take time to explain how to receive eternal life and to pray with your students at this point.

DEPTHFINDER · WHAT IF I DESERVE TO BE JUDGED?

Sometimes discussions like this can trigger appropriate guilt about behaviors kids may see themselves guilty of. It's important for your students to know that you do not judge them for any sins they have repented of—and more importantly, neither does God. Use this passage from Romans 3 to assure kids that just as all people are sinners, so are all people able to be forgiven.

The teenager who feels that his or her sin is "worse" than anyone else's might find comfort in the stories of David's adulterous liaison with Bathsheba and subsequent murder of her husband (2 Samuel 11–12; see also Psalm 51) and Peter's denial of Jesus (Mark 14:27-31, 66-72 and John 21:15-19). Both of these outstanding sinners also became outstanding witnesses of God's grace.

LEADER TIP for Blood Transfusion

To make a visual impact that kids will remember, pass a hospital IV bag around the circle during this closing activity. Surplus stores carry all kinds of medical paraphernalia, or you may be able to get an IV bag from a doctor or nurse in your congregation.

God comes through faith in Jesus Christ to all who believe") and verse 26b ("the one who justifies those who have faith in Jesus"). Point out that in this area, as in others, <u>only God has the right to judge people's hearts.</u>

● **In what way is there "no difference"—as it says in verse 22—between people with AIDS and people without AIDS?**

● **What do you learn about God's justice from this passage?**

Bring kids back together, and form a circle with them. Read aloud the first half of verse 25: **"God presented him [Jesus] as a sacrifice of atonement, through faith in his blood."** Say: **We are all guilty. You might say sin is "in our blood." Jesus' blood is the transfusion that can give eternal life to AIDS patients—and to all of us who are tainted with sin.**

Close by turning to the person next to you in the circle and saying: **God wants to have a relationship with you through Jesus' blood.** Have that person turn to the next person in the circle and say the same words. Have kids pass that assurance all the way around the circle.

Group Studies

Group 1: The Blame Game

1. Read John 9:1-7.
2. In what ways do people ask the same sort of blaming questions today when someone suffers? For example, when someone gets lung cancer, often people will ask, "Was he a smoker?" Choose a contemporary situation, and prepare to dramatize it for the rest of the group. Your drama should include the negative situation (comparable to the man's blindness); the kinds of blaming questions people might ask; and how you think Jesus might respond.

Group 2: Sticks and Stones

1. Read John 8:1-11.
2. Prepare a modern version of this story in which the character is not an adulteress, but someone who contracted AIDS through sexual promiscuity. Be sure to include how people might respond to him or her and Jesus' statement to the accusers.

Group 3: Metaphor Makers

1. Read Matthew 7:1-5.
2. Paraphrase verses 3 and 4, coming up with as many examples as you can to make the same point. For example, "Why do you point out the pimple on your friend's nose, when your whole face is covered with zits?" Write down your examples.

Permission to photocopy this handout from Group's Core Belief Bible Study Series granted for local church use.
Copyright © Group Publishing, Inc., P.O. Box 481, Loveland, CO 80539.

aking a STAND

Putting Obedience to God First

by Julie Meiklejohn

■ Immanuel Oywash was arrested, imprisoned, and fined for breaking the law. His crime? Teaching Christian beliefs against animism, witchcraft, and magic ("Guilty! Christians Fined 2 Cows and 4 Goats," from www.lightsource.net). ■ Bernard Goetz became an American hero overnight. The cause of his popularity? Shooting four teenagers—would-be muggers—on the subway. ■ Oywash broke the law; was he wrong to do so? Goetz broke the law; was he wrong to do so? How do we know? ■ People throughout history have used "justice" as the battle cry behind their actions. In the idealism of adolescence, your kids react strongly against injustice and often feel sympathetic toward causes for justice. They may even be moved to act or refuse to act themselves. ■ But not all cries for "justice" are legitimate. In some cases, civil disobedience may be an appropriate Christian response. In other cases, your kids may be aligning themselves with an incorrect, human view of justice. ■ How can we help kids distinguish between disobedience for the right reasons and disobedience for the wrong reasons? How can we help kids decide when to act and when not to act? ■ God's Word reveals his true justice, and it gives clear guidelines for making good choices. Use this study to give your kids a framework for making good decisions about civil disobedience.

THE POINT:

We're accountable to God for everything we do and don't do.

The Study
AT A GLANCE

SECTION	MINUTES	WHAT STUDENTS WILL DO	SUPPLIES
Investigation	30 to 35	CHOOSE OR LOSE—Participate in a game show about making decisions and research decisions made by people in the Bible.	Bibles, newsprint, markers, tape, "Choose or Lose" chart (p. 49), pencils, paper, "Research Questions" handouts (p. 55)
Application	5 to 10	LIFE'S LITTLE INSTRUCTIONS—Create frameworks to use in decision-making.	Bibles, newsprint, markers, tape
Taking Action	10 to 15	WHAT'S MY CHOICE?—Act out situations in which decisions need to be made and make decisions as a class.	Hat or box, pencils, slips of paper
Commitment	up to 5	DOING THE RIGHT THING—Experience catacomb worship and commit to using God's tools in decision-making.	Small taper candles with drip-catchers, matches

notes:

Permission to photocopy this page from Group's Core Belief Bible Study Series granted for local church use.
Copyright © Group Publishing, Inc., P.O. Box 481, Loveland, CO 80539.

We're accountable to God for everything we do and don't do.

THE BIBLE CONNECTION

EXODUS 1:15-21; 1 SAMUEL 15:1-23; 20:12-42; 2 SAMUEL 15:2-6; 17:1-4; DANIEL 3; JONAH 1; MATTHEW 12:1-14; ACTS 5:17-32	These passages describe situations in which people chose to disobey commands or understood laws.
PSALM 111:7-10; ROMANS 12:1-2; PHILIPPIANS 2:5; JAMES 2:14-17	These passages provide tools for decision-making.

I n this study, kids will participate in a game show about making decisions, research biblical examples of decision-making, create their own systems for making decisions, and put those systems to the test.

Through this participation, kids can discover how to filter information through God's Word, seeking God's view of justice, to decide whether to act and how to act.

LEADER TIP for The Study

Whenever you ask groups to discuss a list of questions, write the list on newsprint, and tape the newsprint to a wall so groups can discuss the questions at their own pace.

BEFORE THE STUDY

On a sheet of newsprint, write the following:
● Group 1
Stories: 1 Samuel 20:12-42 and 2 Samuel 15:2-6; 17:1-4
God's Instructions: Romans 12:1-2
● Group 2
Stories: Exodus 1:15-21 and Daniel 3
God's Instructions: James 2:14-17
● Group 3
Stories: 1 Samuel 15:1-23 and Jonah 1
God's Instructions: Psalm 111:7-10
● Group 4
Stories: Matthew 12:1-14 and Acts 5:17-32
God's Instructions: Philippians 2:5
Tape the newsprint to a wall.
Also make four photocopies of the "Research Questions" handout (p. 55).

THE STUDY

INVESTIGATION ▼

Choose or Lose

(30 to 35 minutes) Have kids form four teams. In your best game-show-host voice, say: **Welcome to Choose or Lose! I'll be your host for our game show today! Choose or Lose is a game of big decisions...and big consequences! In just a few minutes, we'll find out if when you choose, you lose!**

Tell kids that during each team's turn, you will read two newspaper headlines and will summarize two decisions people need to make. Explain that after you read, teams will have ten seconds for each question to decide how the people in the newspaper headlines should react. Tell kids that if a decision matches what really happened, the team will get a point. Say: **While one team is guessing, the rest of you will need to try to influence the team's decision by shouting out the decision you think the team should make. Now, are you ready to choose or lose?**

Choose a team to go first. Using the "Choose or Lose" chart (p. 49), read one of the headlines and consequences out loud, and tell the team it has ten seconds to decide what the people should do. Encourage the other teams to shout out their choices while the team is deciding. After ten seconds, say: **Time's up! What's your choice?** After the team guesses, say: **Correct!** (or **Sorry!**), and read the party's actual decision. Then read the team's second headline and consequence. Continue in this manner until each team has had a chance to decide for two headlines. After each team has had a turn, say: **Congratulations! Let's give the teams who guessed correctly a big round of applause! Those of you who guessed incorrectly, better luck next time!**

Have kids sit down with their groups, and ask:
● **How was making choices in this game similar to making choices in real life? different?**
● **When is making a decision difficult? easy? Why?**

Distribute Bibles to kids and say: **In your groups, research what really happened in the stories we just heard about. Pay close attention to how the characters in the stories decided what to do.** Have groups read their "stories" passages that are listed on the newsprint you prepared before the study. After a few minutes, have kids discuss the following questions in their groups:
● **What happened in each of the stories?**
● **What crucial decision did the people (or person) have to make?**
● **What did the people choose to do? Why?**
● **Do you think the decisions were wise ones or poor ones? Why?**

CHOOSE OR LOSE

Headline	Possible Consequence	The Decision
Team 1—Son Instructed to Capture Father's Enemy	Unless the son complies, he could be disinherited. Does the son comply?	No: The son refuses to hand over his father's enemy (1 Samuel 20:12-42).
Son Undermines Father's Crown	The son could be disinherited or killed if he's discovered. Does the son continue?	Yes: The son increases his efforts to overthrow his father's throne (2 Samuel 15:2-6; 17:1-4).
Team 2—Nurses Ordered to Kill Babies	The nurses could be fired and banished from their country if they refuse. Do the nurses kill the babies?	No: The nurses save the babies (Exodus 1:15-21).
Men Commanded to Worship Statue	The men will be killed if they refuse. Do the men worship the statue?	No: The men refuse to worship the statue, choosing instead to be faithful to God (Daniel 3).
Team 3—King Instructed to Eradicate Town	The king could be forced from his kingdom unless he complies. Does the king comply?	No: The king allows the enemy king and the choicest animals to live (1 Samuel 15:1-23).
Man Ordered to Confront Enemy City	Unless the man obeys, the town's entire population could be harmed. Does the man obey?	No: The man runs away and tries to hide instead (Jonah 1).
Team 4—Teacher Illegally Helps the Sick	If the teacher continues working, he may be killed. Does the teacher continue working?	Yes: The teacher continues his miraculous work (Matthew 12:1-14).
Teachers Ordered to Be Silent	The teachers may be imprisoned if they continue to teach. Do the teachers continue?	Yes: The teachers continue to tell others about Christ (Acts 5:17-32).

● **How did the characters decide what to do? What guidelines did they use?**

Have each group choose a volunteer to summarize the Bible stories and discussion to the rest of the class. Then say: **In each story, someone had to make a decision about whether to disobey a direct command or an understood law. For example, both Jonathan and Absalom disobeyed their fathers, which is not generally the right thing to do. Plus, their fathers were also kings, so they had even more power than a typical dad.** Ask:

● **Do you think Jonathan and Absalom were right or wrong to disobey their fathers? Why?**

Then give each group a pencil and a "Research Questions" handout (p. 55), and give kids about ten minutes to complete their handouts and prepare presentations.

Provide supplies such as newsprint, markers, paper, and pencils for kids to make posters or comics. As kids work, circulate around the room to offer help and answer questions as needed. After about five minutes, encourage kids to start putting together their presentations. Give kids about five minutes to create their presentations. Then have kids present their stories to the whole class.

Then ask:

● **What do you think *you* would have done in any of these situations?**

● **What was the most important consideration for the characters in these stories as they made their decisions?**

● **Through our game and discussion, have you found a common reason that makes it OK to disobey a command or understood law? Explain.**

Say: **When faced with choices like the biblical characters faced, we need to consider God's justice—even if a situation seems unfair. Will our choice honor God, as in the case of Shadrach, Meshach, and Abednego? Will our choice dishonor God, as in the case of Jonah? In each of these stories, the wise decision was a decision for God, and the wrong decision was a decision against God. We are accountable to God for everything we do and don't do.** Let's explore ways we can decide whether or not to take action in situations we may face in our own lives.

APPLICATION ▼

Life's Little Instructions (5 to 10 minutes)

Say: **Sometimes we face tough situations in which we wonder if we should disobey what others are telling us. We can use the situations from our game show or examples from our own lives to create models or systems for making decisions during those tough times. Motivating our choices should be the knowledge that we're accountable to God for everything we do and don't do.** Ask:

● **What are some things we need to remember when we're making decisions?**

Have kids form pairs with others who weren't in their groups before. Give each pair markers, newsprint, and a Bible. Explain that pairs are going to use the supplies to present a system for making Christlike decisions in their own lives. For example, kids could use an acronym such as ACT and assign meaning to each letter: A for "Ask God," C for "Consult the Bible," and T for "Talk to other Christians." Kids could also make posters, bumper stickers, "declarations of decision-making," lists of questions to ask themselves when they're making tough decisions—anything that will help them make Christlike decisions. Say: **As you create your system, keep in mind what we learned in our game and in our discussions about how to make good decisions. Remember that whether or not we decide to act in any situation, our decision needs to be based on God's Word and God's view of**

LEADER TIP for Life's Little Instructions

You may want to write the sample system using the acronym ACT on a chalkboard or newsprint for kids to refer to as they're creating their own systems.

DEPTH FINDER — KIDS AND SOCIAL ACTION

According to Christian speaker and author Anthony Campolo, young people "are attracted to a church that challenges them to do things for others" more than "a church that tries to entertain them." He goes on to say, "Young people just may be looking for a church that appeals to their latent idealism by calling them to be agents of God's revolution and to be part of His movement to bring healing and justice to His broken world...A church which provides its young people with opportunities and challenges for social change gives to them the opportunity to explore some of the primary reasons for their salvation. Through [social action] they will come to see that Jesus is not only interested in saving them from sin and getting them into heaven, but also wants to make them into instruments through which He can do His work in the world...Young people involved in social action will come to understand that God is infinitely concerned with what happens to refugees from Cambodia, the isolated elderly in urban high-rise apartments, the derelicts on skid row, the poor in Appalachia, and the victims of racial segregation. They will come to know a God who is angry when a multinational corporation pursues exploitive policies...which serve special interest groups at the expense of the poor. They would come to understand that God is one who is joyful when there are opportunities for oppressed people to gain dignity. In short, social action programs help young people to understand something of the nature of God and to gain an understanding of why God chose to save them from sin and make them into new creatures."

(Anthony Campolo, *Ideas for Social Action*)

justice because <u>we're accountable to God for everything we do and don't do.</u>

Give pairs about five minutes to come up with their systems, and then have each pair share its system with the class. Tape the systems to a wall so kids can refer to them during the next activity.

TAKING ACTION ▼

What's My Choice? (10 to 15 minutes) Have kids form new groups of four, and give each group a pencil and a slip of paper. Say: <u>We're accountable to God for everything we do and don't do,</u> and God gives us several ways to discover his will in every situation, including prayer, reading the Bible, and discussing situations with other Christians. Keeping that in mind, let's put the systems you created to work.

Ask each group to think of one situation they may face in their lives that may or may not require them to act in order to help effect God's justice. An example situation might be: "If a teacher during a class proclaims himself to be an atheist and openly antagonizes you and your Christian friends for believing in Christ, what should you do?" Have each group write its situation on a slip of paper; after a minute, collect the slips of paper and put them into a hat or a box.

LEADER TIP for What's My Choice?

If kids are having trouble thinking of situations, here are a few suggestions:
● A group of students at school is being discriminated against by other students and some teachers because of their ethnic background. You want to do something to change the situation.
● You are an exchange student in a country where owning a Bible is against the law. You meet a budding Christian who wants a Bible.
● A factory in your city is polluting a river with its waste. You and a group of your friends want to do something about it.

DEPTHFINDER
MARTIN LUTHER KING JR.

Martin Luther King Jr.'s message of justice, peace, and human dignity came from combining Christian pacifism with "getting things done." His leadership from the pulpit, at the podium, and in the streets involved millions in the nonviolent movement for racial equality that helped shatter the American system of segregation.

In 1955, when the Montgomery bus boycott was picking up steam, King and other boycott leaders were called to task by several white ministers, who felt that they should be preaching only the Gospel rather than "sowing confusion by getting enmeshed in social problems." In response, King stated:

"We believe firmly in the revelation of God in Jesus Christ. I can see no conflict between our devotion to Jesus Christ and our present action. In fact, I can see a necessary relationship. If one is truly devoted to the religion of Jesus, he will seek to rid the earth of social evils. The gospel is social as well as personal...As Christians we owe our ultimate allegiance to God and His Will, rather than to man and his folkways."

(Let the Trumpet Sound by Stephen B. Oates, as quoted in *The Scattered Voice* by James W. Skillen)

Then have each group draw a slip of paper from the hat or box. If a group draws its own situation, have it draw again and put its own situation back. Then say: **You have three minutes to create a short skit which presents the situation but doesn't present a decision or the ending. Make sure your skit involves each person in your group (you may need to add characters), and remember not to show an ending.** After three minutes, say: **Time's up! Now as each**

"If we are thrown into the blazing furnace, the God we serve is able to save us from it, and he will rescue us from your hand, **O king. But** even if he does not, we want you to know, **O king,** that we will not serve your gods or worship the image of gold you have set up."
—Daniel 3:17-18

DEPTH FINDER — RELIGIOUS PERSECUTION

After Jesus' death, many Christians were persecuted for their faith. Christians faced the possibility of many different types of persecution, including imprisonment and death.

Today, although we as Americans have the inalienable right to worship as we choose, religious persecution is still very much a problem in other parts of the world. According to a U.S. State Department Report, "Christians are subject to difficulties ranging from interference to outright persecution in many countries, including Iraq, Pakistan, and the Sudan." The study also listed Saudi Arabia, Vietnam, Germany, China, Nigeria, Cuba, and Burma as countries in which human rights conditions were deplorable.

In response to the report, Secretary of State Madeleine Albright committed to fight such persecution. She stated, "These are plagues that, from ancient times, have fomented war and deep-seated resentment. Whatever your culture, whatever your creed, the right to worship is basic."

("Religious Persecution Still a Global Issue," The Denver Post, February 1, 1997)

group performs its skit, the rest of you will need to be thinking about the situation and the systems for decision-making that are hanging on the wall. Explain that after each skit ends, the rest of the class will discuss the situation and decide what to do based on the decision-making systems. Tell kids that once they've made a decision, the group will finish the skit by acting out an ending based on the decision. Remind kids that inaction is also a valid decision—sometimes the best decision.

Have each group act out its situation; then have the rest of the class discuss the situation and make a decision based on the systems for the group to act out.

When all of the groups have acted out their situations, ask:

● **Did you find it easy or difficult to decide how to end these skits? Explain.**

● **Did the systems for decision-making help you decide what to do? Why or why not?**

● **Can you think of situations in your own life in which you could apply these systems?**

● **When is it OK to disobey? Explain.**

● **When is it definitely not OK to disobey? Explain.**

● **How can thinking ahead of time about how to make a choice help you make the right choice?**

Say: <u>We are accountable to God for everything we do and don't do,</u> and God will help us make good decisions in every situation.

LEADER TIP for Doing the Right Thing

You may want to pass out index cards or slips of paper and have kids copy the systems for decision-making to take home with them.

Doing the Right Thing
(up to 5 minutes)

Say: **As we heard earlier in one of the Bible stories, it was against the law for early Christians to worship God. They risked imprisonment or even death. It's thought that many early Christians hid in catacombs, or tombs, to worship secretly. They had no Bibles or songbooks, and often the leaders of their communities were in prison or had been killed. To close our study today, we're going to simulate catacomb worship.** Give each student a small candle with a drip-catcher, and turn out the lights in your classroom.

Have students gather close together in one corner of the classroom.

Say: **We're accountable to God for everything we do and don't do. God gives us many tools that we can use in making difficult decisions, such as prayer, Bible study, and conversations with other Christians. God expects us to use these tools in any decision we must make. Now I'd like you to think of one specific thing you can commit to in the coming weeks which will help you to make good decisions. One example is reading and studying the Bible.** Give kids a few seconds to think of something they want to commit to. Then say: **Now we're going to share our commitments with God and each other. I'll light my candle and share my commitment aloud. Then I'll light the next person's candle. As that person lights the next person's candle, he or she will say, "To help me be accountable to God in my decisions, I will..."**

After everyone has shared a commitment, have each person turn to a partner and tell that person one quality he or she has which can help with decision-making. Close with a prayer, asking God to help kids make good decisions and act according to his will.

Research Questions?

Use about five minutes to answer these questions using the "God's Instructions" passages listed for your group on the sheet of newsprint.

1. Briefly summarize your "God's Instructions" passage.

2. What does this passage tell you about how God wants us to make decisions?

3. How could the characters in your stories have used this knowledge as they made their decisions?

Now think of a creative way for your group to present to the class the information you've discovered. For example, you could make a poster, do a short skit, or draw a cartoon. In your presentations, be sure to include a short summary of God's instructions and an explanation of whether the characters in the stories were motivated by faith in God or by something else. You have five minutes to prepare your presentation.

Permission to photocopy this handout from Group's Core Belief Bible Study Series granted for local church use.
Copyright © Group Publishing, Inc., P.O. Box 481, Loveland, CO 80539.

why ▼ Active and Interactive Learning works with teenagers

Let's Start With the Big Picture

Think back to a major life lesson you've learned.
Got it? Now answer these questions:
- Did you learn your lesson from something you read?
- Did you learn it from something you heard?
- Did you learn it from something you experienced?

If you're like 99 percent of your peers, you answered "yes" only to the third question—you learned your life lesson from something you experienced.

This simple test illustrates the most convincing reason for using active and interactive learning with young people: People learn best through experience. Or to put it even more simply, people learn by doing.

Learning by doing is what active learning is all about. No more sitting quietly in chairs and listening to a speaker expound theories about God—that's passive learning. Active learning gets kids out of their chairs and into the experience of life. With active learning, kids get to *do* what they're studying. They *feel* the effects of the principles you teach. They *learn* by experiencing truth firsthand.

Active learning works because it recognizes three basic learning needs and uses them in concert to enable young people to make discoveries on their own and to find practical life applications for the truths they believe.

So what are these three basic learning needs?
1. Teenagers need action.
2. Teenagers need to think.
3. Teenagers need to talk.

Read on to find out exactly how these needs will be met by using the active and interactive learning techniques in Group's Core Belief Bible Study Series in your youth group.

1. Teenagers Need Action

Aircraft pilots know well the difference between passive and active learning. Their passive learning comes through listening to flight instructors and reading flight-instruction books. Their active learning comes through actually flying an airplane or flight simulator. Books and lectures may be helpful, but pilots really learn to fly by manipulating a plane's controls themselves.

We can help young people learn in a similar way. Though we may engage students passively in some reading and listening to teachers, their understanding and application of God's Word will really take off through simulated and real-life experiences.

Forms of active learning include simulation games; role-plays; service projects; experiments; research projects; group pantomimes; mock trials; construction projects; purposeful games; field trips; and, of course, the most powerful form of active learning—real-life experiences.

We can more fully explain active learning by exploring four of its characteristics:

● **Active learning is an adventure.** Passive learning is almost always predictable. Students sit passively while the teacher or speaker follows a planned outline or script.

In active learning, kids may learn lessons the teacher never envisioned. Because the leader trusts students to help create the learning experience, learners may venture into unforeseen discoveries. And often the teacher learns as much as the students.

● **Active learning is fun and captivating.** What are we communicating when we say, "OK, the fun's over—time to talk about God"? What's the hidden message? That joy is separate from God? And that learning is separate from joy?

What a shame.

Active learning is not joyless. One seventh-grader we interviewed clearly remembered her best Sunday school lesson: "Jesus was the light, and we went into a dark room and shut off the lights. We had a candle, and we learned that Jesus is the light and the dark can't shut off the light." That's active learning. Deena enjoyed the lesson. She had fun. And she learned.

Active learning intrigues people. Whether they find a foot-washing experience captivating or maybe a bit uncomfortable, they learn. And they learn on a level deeper than any work sheet or teacher's lecture could ever reach.

● **Active learning involves everyone.** Here the difference between passive and active learning becomes abundantly clear. It's like the difference between watching a football game on television and actually playing in the game.

The "trust walk" provides a good example of involving everyone in active learning. Half of the group members put on blindfolds; the other half serve as guides. The "blind" people trust the guides to lead them through the building or outdoors. The guides prevent the blind people from falling down stairs or tripping over rocks. Everyone needs to participate to learn the inherent lessons of trust, faith, doubt, fear, confidence, and servanthood. Passive spectators of this experience would learn little, but participants learn a great deal.

● **Active learning is focused through debriefing.** Activity simply for activity's sake doesn't usually result in good learning. Debriefing— evaluating an experience by discussing it in pairs or small groups— helps focus the experience and draw out its meaning. Debriefing helps sort and order the information students gather during the experience. It helps learners relate the recently experienced activity to their lives.

The process of debriefing is best started immediately after an experience. We use a three-step process in debriefing: reflection, interpretation, and application.

Reflection—This first step asks the students, "How did you feel?" Active-learning experiences typically evoke an emotional reaction, so it's appropriate to begin debriefing at that level.

Some people ask, "What do feelings have to do with education?" Feelings have everything to do with education. Think back again to that time in your life when you learned a big lesson. In all likelihood, strong feelings accompanied that lesson. Our emotions tend to cement things into our memories.

When you're debriefing, use open-ended questions to probe feelings. Avoid questions that can be answered with a "yes" or "no." Let your learners know that there are no wrong answers to these "feeling" questions. Everyone's feelings are valid.

Interpretation—The next step in the debriefing process asks, "What does this mean to you? How is this experience like or unlike some other aspect of your life?" Now you're asking people to identify a message or principle from the experience.

You want your learners to discover the message for themselves. So instead of telling students your answers, take the time to ask questions that encourage self-discovery. Use Scripture and discussion in pairs or small groups to explore how the actions and effects of the activity might translate to their lives.

Alert! Some of your people may interpret wonderful messages that you never intended. That's not failure! That's the Holy Spirit at work. God allows us to catch different glimpses of his kingdom even when we all look through the same glass.

Application—The final debriefing step asks, "What will you do about it?" This step moves learning into action. Your young people have shared a common experience. They've discovered a principle. Now they must create something new with what they've just experienced and interpreted. They must integrate the message into their lives.

The application stage of debriefing calls for a decision. Ask your students how they'll change, how they'll grow, what they'll do as a result of your time together.

2. Teenagers Need to Think

Today's students have been trained not to think. They aren't dumber than previous generations. We've simply conditioned them not to use their heads.

You see, we've trained our kids to respond with the simplistic answers they think the teacher wants to hear. Fill-in-the-blank student workbooks and teachers who ask dead-end questions such as "What's the capital of Delaware?" have produced kids and adults who have learned not to think.

And it doesn't just happen in junior high or high school. Our children are schooled very early not to think. Teachers attempt to help kids read with nonsensical fill-in-the-blank drills, word scrambles, and missing-letter puzzles.

Helping teenagers think requires a paradigm shift in how we teach. We need to plan for and set aside time for higher-order thinking and be willing to reduce our time spent on lower-order parroting. Group's Core Belief Bible Study Series is designed to help you do just that.

Thinking classrooms look quite different from traditional classrooms. In most church environments, the teacher does most of the talking and hopes that knowledge will transmit from his or her brain to the students'. In thinking settings, the teacher coaches students to ponder, wonder, imagine, and problem-solve.

3. Teenagers Need to Talk

Everyone knows that the person who learns the most in any class is the teacher. Explaining a concept to someone else is usually more helpful to the explainer than to the listener. So why not let the students do more teaching? That's one of the chief benefits of letting kids do the talking. This process is called interactive learning.

What is interactive learning? Interactive learning occurs when students discuss and work cooperatively in pairs or small groups.

Interactive learning encourages learners to work together. It honors the fact that students can learn from one another, not just from the teacher. Students work together in pairs or small groups to accomplish shared goals. They build together, discuss together, and present together. They teach each other and learn from one another. Success as a group is celebrated. Positive interdependence promotes individual and group learning.

Interactive learning not only helps people learn but also helps learners feel better about themselves and get along better with others. It accomplishes these things more effectively than the independent or competitive methods.

Here's a selection of interactive learning techniques that are used in Group's Core Belief Bible Study Series. With any of these models, leaders may assign students to specific partners or small groups. This will maximize cooperation and learning by preventing all the "rowdies" from linking up. And it will allow for new friendships to form outside of established cliques.

Following any period of partner or small-group work, the leader may reconvene the entire class for large-group processing. During this time the teacher may ask for reports or discoveries from individuals or teams. This technique builds in accountability for the teacherless pairs and small groups.

Pair-Share—With this technique each student turns to a partner and responds to a question or problem from the teacher or leader. Every learner responds. There are no passive observers. The teacher may then ask people to share their partners' responses.

Study Partners—Most curricula and most teachers call for Scripture passages to be read to the whole class by one person. One reads; the others doze.

Why not relinquish some teacher control and let partners read and react with each other? They'll all be involved—and will learn more.

Learning Groups—Students work together in small groups to create a model, design artwork, or study a passage or story; then they discuss what they learned through the experience. Each person in the learning group may be assigned a specific role. Here are some examples:

Reader

Recorder (makes notes of key thoughts expressed during the reading or discussion)

Checker (makes sure everyone understands and agrees with answers arrived at by the group)

Encourager (urges silent members to share their thoughts)

When everyone has a specific responsibility, knows what it is, and contributes to a small group, much is accomplished and much is learned.

Summary Partners—One student reads a paragraph, then the partner summarizes the paragraph or interprets its meaning. Partners alternate roles with each paragraph.

The paraphrasing technique also works well in discussions. Anyone who wishes to share a thought must first paraphrase what the previous person said. This sharpens listening skills and demonstrates the power of feedback communication.

Jigsaw—Each person in a small group examines a different concept, Scripture, or part of an issue. Then each teaches the others in the group. Thus, all members teach, and all must learn the others' discoveries. This technique is called a jigsaw because individuals are responsible to their group for different pieces of the puzzle.

JIGSAW EXAMPLE

Here's an example of a jigsaw.

Assign four-person teams. Have teammates each number off from one to four. Have all the Ones go to one corner of the room, all the Twos to another corner, and so on.

Tell team members they're responsible for learning information in their numbered corners and then for teaching their team members when they return to their original teams.

Give the following assignments to various groups:

Ones: Read Psalm 22. Discuss and list the prophecies made about Jesus.

Twos: Read Isaiah 52:13—53:12. Discuss and list the prophecies made about Jesus.

Threes: Read Matthew 27:1-32. Discuss and list the things that happened to Jesus.

Fours: Read Matthew 27:33-66. Discuss and list the things that happened to Jesus.

After the corner groups meet and discuss, instruct all learners to return to their original teams and report what they've learned. Then have each team determine which prophecies about Jesus were fulfilled in the passages from Matthew.

Call on various individuals in each team to report one or two prophecies that were fulfilled.

You Can Do It Too!

All this information may sound revolutionary to you, but it's really not. God has been using active and interactive learning to teach his people for generations. Just look at Abraham and Isaac, Jacob and Esau, Moses and the Israelites, Ruth and Boaz. And then there's Jesus, who used active learning all the time!

Group's Core Belief Bible Study Series makes it easy for you to use active and interactive learning with your group. The active and interactive elements are automatically built in! Just follow the outlines, and watch as your kids grow through experience and positive interaction with others.

FOR DEEPER STUDY

For more information on incorporating active and interactive learning into your work with teenagers, check out these resources:

● *Why Nobody Learns Much of Anything at Church: And How to Fix It,* by Thom and Joani Schultz (Group Publishing) and
● *Do It! Active Learning in Youth Ministry,* by Thom and Joani Schultz (Group Publishing).

your evaluation of

Bible Study Series
for senior high

why
GOD'S JUSTICE matters

Group Publishing, Inc.
Attention: Core Belief Talk-Back
P.O. Box 481
Loveland, CO 80539
Fax: (970) 669-1994

Please help us continue to provide innovative and useful resources for ministry. After you've led the studies in this volume, take a moment to fill out this evaluation; then mail or fax it to us at the address above. Thanks!

● ● ● ● ● ●

1. As a whole, this book has been (circle one)

not very helpful   very helpful
1   2   3   4   5   6   7   8   9   10

2. The best things about this book:

3. How this book could be improved:

4. What I will change because of this book:

5. Would you be interested in field-testing future Core Belief Bible Studies and giving us your feedback? If so, please complete the information below:

Name _____

Street address _____

City _____ State _____ Zip _____

Daytime telephone (____) _____ Date _____

THANKS!

Permission to photocopy this evaluation from Group's Core Belief Bible Study Series granted for local church use.
Copyright © Group Publishing, Inc., P.O. Box 481, Loveland, CO 80539.